GW01191721

Oxford and Cambridge
Level Boosters
English

Age 10–11

Contents

How these tests will help your child

These tests are designed for use with children in Year 6 (aged 10–11 years). They will:

Firstly let you compare your child's performance in English against the levels expected for children of his or her age.

Secondly show your child's particular strengths and weaknesses in English, enabling you to work together with your child to improve and achieve better results in the future.

Two tests are included for use at different times, so that you can measure progress. We suggest that you use the first test before March to find out how well your child is doing, and also how he or she can work to improve. The second test can then be used at the beginning of May to check on the progress made and (if necessary) to identify any remaining problems.

Success by design

Most other tests that you will find in the shops have been written to mimic the national tests, but they have not been through the rigorous development processes used in national test development. The tests in this book are different. They are carefully constructed to make them easy to use at home and to give you accurate information. They have been:

- specially designed for home use

- written by experts who develop, research and mark National Curriculum tests

- produced in multiple-choice format for straightforward and accurate marking

- designed to provide a detailed breakdown of your child's knowledge and understanding

- tried and tested with large numbers of children

- calibrated against actual national levels

- written so that you can find how to help when your child gets answers wrong.

Taking the tests

What you will need

Remove the marking sheet from the middle of this booklet for later use.

Your child will need a pencil or a pen. No other aids are needed.

He or she should work in a quiet room where it is possible to concentrate.

- Bedrooms are not usually the best place; a dining or kitchen table is often better.

- Make sure other people do not walk into the room.

What to do

Make sure your child feels relaxed and confident. Spend a few minutes looking through the booklet together. These tests can, and should, be enjoyable. It will help to point out that *some of the questions are bound to be difficult* and *not to worry* about this, but just to *have a go*.

If this is the first time your child has used these tests, read through the practice question on page 6 together. After this, your child should work independently. You should not read out the passages or questions to your child.

There is *no time limit* for these tests. It is important for the correct use of the tests that children try to answer as many of the questions as they can. Each 50-mark test should take about one hour to complete. If children take much longer than this, it is a sign that they may not be working as fast as would be expected in the national tests. Take care that your child does not get too tired. You may wish to spread one test over two sessions.

The information in the centre pull-out section tells you how to mark the tests. On page 49 you will find guidance on how well your child is doing.

The National Curriculum

The National Curriculum sets out what must be taught in schools at each key stage. It also sets out what pupils are expected to achieve as a result of this teaching. The National Literacy Strategy indicates what should be taught in each year.

Programmes of study

Each curriculum subject has a 'programme of study' that says what should be taught to pupils.

The National Curriculum for English covers *Speaking and Listening, Reading,* and *Writing,* which includes handwriting and spelling. A wide range of knowledge, understanding and skills is taught within these areas of study.

Doing your level best

For each of the main curriculum subjects, there are eight levels of performance. Children are expected to move up about one level every two years. So by the time they are 11 years old most children are expected to have reached level 4. Some children will do better, while a few will not achieve this level. The diagram below shows the range of attainment at the end of each year in Key Stage 2 (ages 7–11 years).

Attainment over Key Stage 2

	Year 3 (age 7–8)	Year 4 (age 8–9)	Year 5 (age 9–10)	Year 6 (age 10–11)
Very few children are at this level, and they generally need extra learning support				
A few children are at this level, which is just below the expected level of attainment	Level 1	Level 1	Level 1	Level 1
	Level 2	Level 2	Level 2	Level 2
The large majority of children should reach this level				
A few children reach this level, which is above the expected level of attainment	Level 3	Level 3	Level 3	Level 3
	Level 4	Level 4	Level 4	Level 4
	Level 5	Level 5	Level 5	Level 5

Very small numbers of exceptional children will reach levels outside the shaded range.

Levels of attainment are measured in school by two different means. At the ages of 7, 11 and 14, pupils take national tests in the main subjects (some people call them 'SATs'). These give a 'snapshot' of what children can do at one point in time. For English, at the end of Key Stage 2 (age 11) children are tested in *Reading* and *Writing*. The results have to be reported to parents.

Teachers also carry out their own assessments of pupils against the same attainment targets, and the results are reported alongside the national test results. Teacher assessment gives a fuller picture of how pupils are doing, as it is not confined to a single 'snapshot'. It can also cover things that are not included in the tests.

There are no compulsory national tests for children at other ages. However, there are optional tests in English and mathematics that schools can choose to use at ages 8, 9 and 10 years. These allow teachers to check children's progress against a national picture, and are widely used. These results are often reported to parents.

How these tests are designed

Each test in this series has been carefully put together to give high-quality information about children's attainment. The tests are intended for use at specific ages, and the content of each test has been selected to match closely what the National Literacy Strategy says children should be taught up to that particular year.

The English tests are each designed around short reading passages selected according to the same stringent criteria used in national test development. These give a good spread of reading material. For each 50-mark test there are:

- two fiction passages, with accompanying questions based on reading and understanding

- two non-fiction passages, with accompanying questions on finding answers from the information

- questions on spelling, related to the reading passages.

Each question is focused at a particular National Curriculum level. Over the whole test, a balance of questions has been used, so that most children will find some questions easy and other questions more challenging. The majority of questions are pitched at the levels that most children of that age are expected to be working at. The following table shows how the level of challenge increases gradually over the the series of four books.

Number of marks at:	Year 3 (age 7–8)	Year 4 (age 8–9)	Year 5 (age 9–10)	Year 6 (age 10–11)
Level 2	38	31	12	4
Level 3	60	55	49	25
Level 4	2	14	35	54
Level 5	–	–	4	17
Total marks in the two tests:	*100*	*100*	*100*	*100*

Practice question

The test is in four parts. Each part starts with a reading passage. Read the passage carefully before answering the questions. You will need to look back at the passage from time to time as you work on the questions.

Each question has four possible answers, marked **A, B, C, D**. Circle the letter to show the correct answer, like this.

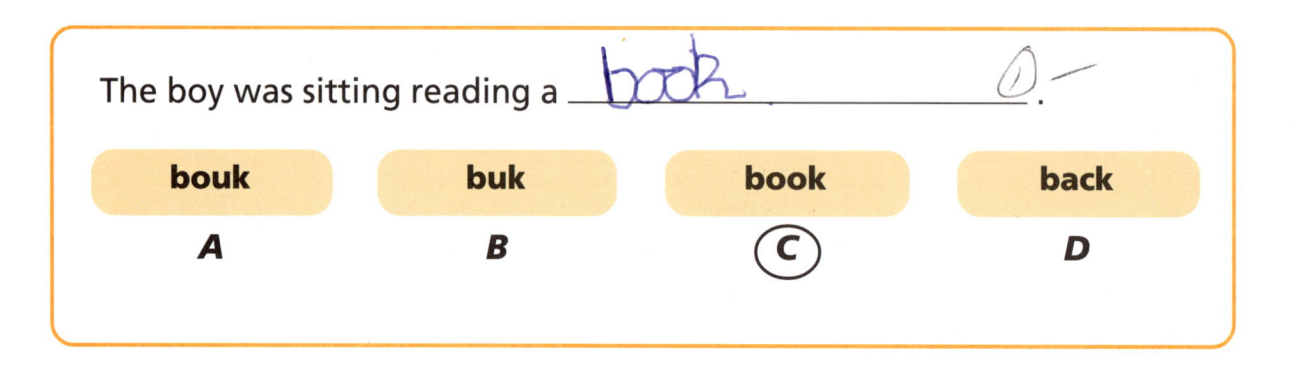

Try to answer all the questions. Work as quickly as you can, but don't rush.

If you make a mistake, cross out your answer and circle the letter for the correct answer.

Test 1

Robert Westall

THE KINGDOM BY THE SEA

HE WAS AN OLD HAND at air raids now. As the yell of the siren climbed the sky, he came smoothly out of his dreams. Not scared. Only his stomach clamped down tight for action, as his hands found his clothes laid ready in the dark. Hauled one jumper, then another, over his pyjamas. Thrust both stockinged feet together through his trousers and into his shoes. Then bent to tie his laces thoroughly. A loose lace had tripped him once, in the race to the shelter. He remembered the smashing blow as the ground hit his chin; the painful week after, not able to eat with a bitten tongue.

He grabbed his school raincoat off the door, pulling the door wide at the same time. All done by feel; no need to put the light on. Lights were dangerous.

He passed Dulcie's door, heard Mam and Dulcie muttering to each other, Dulcie sleepy and cross, Mam sharp and urgent. Then he thundered downstairs; the crack of light from the kitchen door lighting up the edge of each stair-tread. Dad was sitting in his warden's uniform, hauling on his big black boots, his grey hair standing up vertically in a bunch, like a cock's comb. Without looking up, Dad said, "Not again! Four nights in a row!"

There was a strong smell of Dad's sweaty feet, and the fag he had burning in the ashtray.

That was all Harry had time to notice; he had his own job: the two objects laid ready in the chair by the door. The big roll of blankets, wrapped in a groundsheet because the shelter was damp, done up with a big leather strap of Dad's. And Mam's precious attache case with the flask of hot coffee and insurance policies and other important things, and the little bottle of brandy for emergencies. He heaved the blankets on to his back, picked up the case with one hand and reached to unlock the back door with the other.

"Mind that light," said Dad automatically. But Harry's hand was already reaching for the switch. He'd done it all a hundred times before.

He slammed the door behind him, held his breath and listened. A single aircraft's engines, far out to sea. *Vroomah, vroomah, vroomah.* But nothing to worry about yet. Two guns fired, one after another. Two brilliant points of white, lighting up a black landscape of greenhouse, sweet-pea trellises and cucumber-frames. A rolling carpet of echoes. Still out to sea. Safe, then.

He ran down the long back garden, with his neck prickling and the blankets bouncing against his back comfortingly. As he passed the greenhouse the rabbits thumped their heels in alarm. There was a nice cold smell of dew and cabbages. Then he was in through the shelter door, shoving the damp mould-stinking curtain aside.

1 How did Harry feel when the air raid started?

He was calm.	**He was pleased.**
A	B
He was surprised.	**He was terrified.**
C	D

He was calm.

2 What clothing did Harry put on?

Ross

jumper, socks and shoes	**pyjamas, shoes, jumpers**
A	B
school uniform, jumper, shoes	**trousers, two jumpers, shoes, raincoat**
C	D

Stacy

Harry put on his pyjamas, shoes, jumpers.

3 How had Harry hurt his chin?

He bit his tongue.	**He fell over his shoelace.**
A	B
He was hit.	**Someone tripped him up.**
C	D

Harry fell and tripped up.

4 Why do you think Dulcie is cross?

She doesn't like being woken up.	**She doesn't like the light on.**
A	B
She has hurt herself.	**She is being told off.**
C	D

Dulcie doesn't like being woken up.

5 Harry 'thundered' down the stairs. How did he move?

loudly and carefully	quickly and calmly
A	**B**

quickly and noisily	quickly and quietly
C	**D**

Harry moved quickly and noisily.

6 Dad's hair was 'like a cock's comb'. How did it look?

he didn't have much hair	sticking out at the sides
A	**B**

sticking up in a line	thin and untidy
C	**D**

Dads (Harry) hair was thin and untidy.

7 Why would the family take 'important things' to the shelter?

A because they were running away

B in case of burglars

C in case the house was bombed

D ready for their journey

8 'He'd done it all a hundred times before.' Which word has 'd replaced in this sentence?

did	had	should	would
A	**B**	**C**	**D**

9 Why did Dad say, "Mind that light"?

to make sure Harry turned it off	**to make sure Harry turned it on**
A	*B*
to make sure it stayed off	**to make sure it stayed on**
C	*D*

B × To make sure it stayed off.

10 How would you describe Harry's behaviour during the night-time air raid?

annoyed	**excited**
A	*B*
frightened	**organised**
C	*D*

Harry was annoyed

11 The first aeroplane to fly ___Successfully___ was a biplane built by Orville and Wilbur Wright.

successfuly	**succesfully**
A	*B*
successfully	**sucsessfuly**
C	*D*

12 As knowledge of structure and ___aerodynamic___ improved, the biplane was gradually replaced by the monoplane.

aerodinamics	**aerodynamics**
A	*B*
aerdynamix	**airodynamics**
C	*D*

from *Crazy Kites* by Peter Eldin

LET'S GO AND FLY A KITE

THE ORIGIN OF THE KITE

It is said that the kite was invented by a Chinese farmer whose hat kept blowing off in the wind. To avoid losing it completely he tied a string to it. It blew off his head, but instead of bowling along the ground as before, it flew up into the air and cavorted at the end of the string. And that, according to Chinese legend, is how the kite was born.

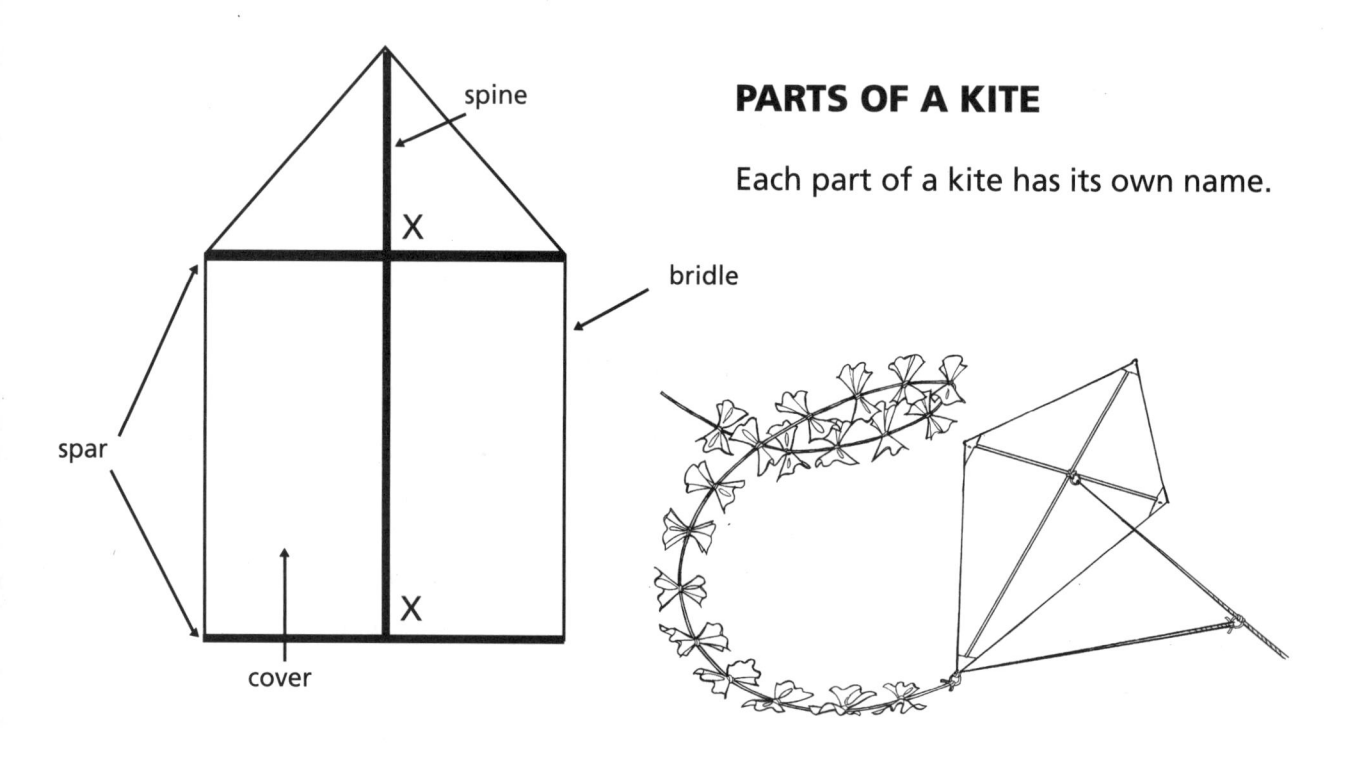

PARTS OF A KITE

Each part of a kite has its own name.

DOS AND DON'TS OF KITE FLYING

◆ Always wear gloves when flying a kite as you can burn or cut your hands with the string.

◆ Do not fly your kite across a road or a railway line.

◆ Keep well away from power lines.

◆ Remember it is against the law in Britain to fly a kite at a height of more than 60 metres.

◆ Never fly a kite in a thunderstorm.

HOW TO MAKE A KITE

The Serpent

You will need:	a **spine**, 50cm long
	2 **spars**, 35cm long
	string
	glue
	wrapping paper
	crepe paper
	paints.

1. Attach one **spar** to the base of the **spine** and the other 10cm down from the top of the spine.

2. Wrapping paper is used for the **cover**. Cut it slightly larger than is required and then fold down around the frame and glue the edges to make them a bit stronger. This is the head of the serpent.

3. Make a tail of one continuous length of crepe paper about 8 metres long. Cut the tail so that it is 20cm wide at the head end and narrow it gradually all the way down its length until it tapers off to a point at the far end.

4. Attach a two-legged **bridle** at the points marked X.

5. Decorate the head with the face of a serpent. This can be ferocious or funny – it is up to you.

6. Decorate the tail with stripes of a zigzag pattern to give the whole kite a snake-like appearance.

13 'It is said that the kite was invented by a Chinese farmer.'
This is

a fact.	an announcement.	a rumour.	a speech.
A	**B**	**C**	**D**

14 Why did the farmer tie a string to his hat?

to keep it on his head	to make a kite
A	**B**

to prevent it blowing away completely	to stop it falling off
C	**D**

15 'It flew up into the air and cavorted at the end of the string.'
What does *cavorted* mean?

escaped	leaped about
A	**B**

spun wildly	tugged hard
C	**D**

16 Which answer gives two correct pieces of advice about kite flying?

A Keep away from power lines.

B Keep away from traffic and fly it as high as you can.

C Wear gloves and find a safe open space.

D When there are thunderstorms and wind it is dangerous to fly a kite.

17 There are six instructions on how to make a kite. Five of the instructions begin with

an adjective.	a noun.	a pronoun.	a verb.
A	**B**	**C**	**D**

18 Some of the words in the instructions are printed in bold lettering. This is because

they are difficult words.	they are important.
A	**B**
they refer to parts shown in the diagram.	they refer to the subheadings.
C	**D**

19 In the instructions what is the glue used for?

to fix on the head	to fasten on the tail
A	**B**
to join the frame	to stick and strengthen the cover
C	**D**

20 In instruction number 3, what words could replace *tapers*?

becomes narrower	becomes thicker
A	**B**
comes to an end	gets shorter
C	**D**

21 20cm means 20 centimetres. The *cm* is

an abbreviation.	a contraction.	a label.	a symbol.
A	**B**	**C**	**D**

22 'This can be ferocious or funny – it is up to you.' *It is up to you* means that this is

a request. A	**a suggestion.** B
an instruction. C	**an invitation.** D

23 In the instructions, when should you decorate the tail?

after you decorate the head A	**before you make the bridle** B
in instruction number 3 C	**when you cut the paper** D

24 The great Italian traveller Marco Polo came back from China and _____ huge kites that hoisted prisoners into the air.

discribed A	**descriebd** B
described C	**deskribed** D

25 The hang-glider is the cheapest and simplest form of aircraft, and hang-gliding is an _____ popular sport.

increasingly A	**increasingley** B
increesingly C	**increasinglly** D

Total (14)

Malorie Blackman

CAM THE HEART BOY
from *Pig Heart Boy*

The noise was deafening. Shouting, screaming, laughing, shrieking – it was thunderous. I thought my head was about to explode. I took a deep breath, breathed out, inhaled again, then dipped down until my head was completely under water.

Silence.

Peace.

It was like a radio being switched off. I sat down at the bottom of the swimming pool and opened my eyes. The chlorine in the water stung, but better that than not seeing what was coming and being kicked in the face. I would've liked to stay down there for ever, but within seconds my lungs were aching and there came a sharp, stabbing pain in my chest. My blood roared like some kind of angry monster in my ears.

I closed my eyes and stood up slowly. If I had to emerge, it would be at my own pace and in my own time – no matter how much my body screamed at me to take a breath as fast as I could. I was the one in control. Not my lungs. Not my blood. Not my heart.

"Cam, are you all right?"

I opened my eyes. Marlon stood in front of me, his green eyes dark and huge with concern. I inhaled sharply, waiting for the roaring in my ears to subside. The pain in my chest took a little longer. "Course! I'm fine," I replied a little breathlessly.

"What were you doing?"

"Just sitting down."

Marlon frowned. "Is that smart?"

"I was just sitting down. Don't fuss. Sometimes you're worse than Mum and Dad," I said.

"If your parents find out that you're here every Tuesday instead of at my house, I'm terrified some grown-up who knows your family is going to spot you and tell your parents." Marlon looked around the pool anxiously, as if expecting his words to come true at that precise moment.

"Marlon, you worry too much." My smile broadened as the pain in my chest lessened.

"How long were you under water?"

"A few seconds. Why?"

"I really don't think you should..."

I'd had enough. "Marlon, bog off!" I snapped. "You're getting on my last nerve now!"

"I was just..."

"I know what you were doing, and you can stop it," I said firmly. "You're beginning to cheese me off."

Marlon clamped his lips together tight and looked away. He was hurt and we both knew it. I fought down the urge to apologise. Why should I say I was sorry? Marlon knew how much I hated to be clucked over. But, as always, I caved in.

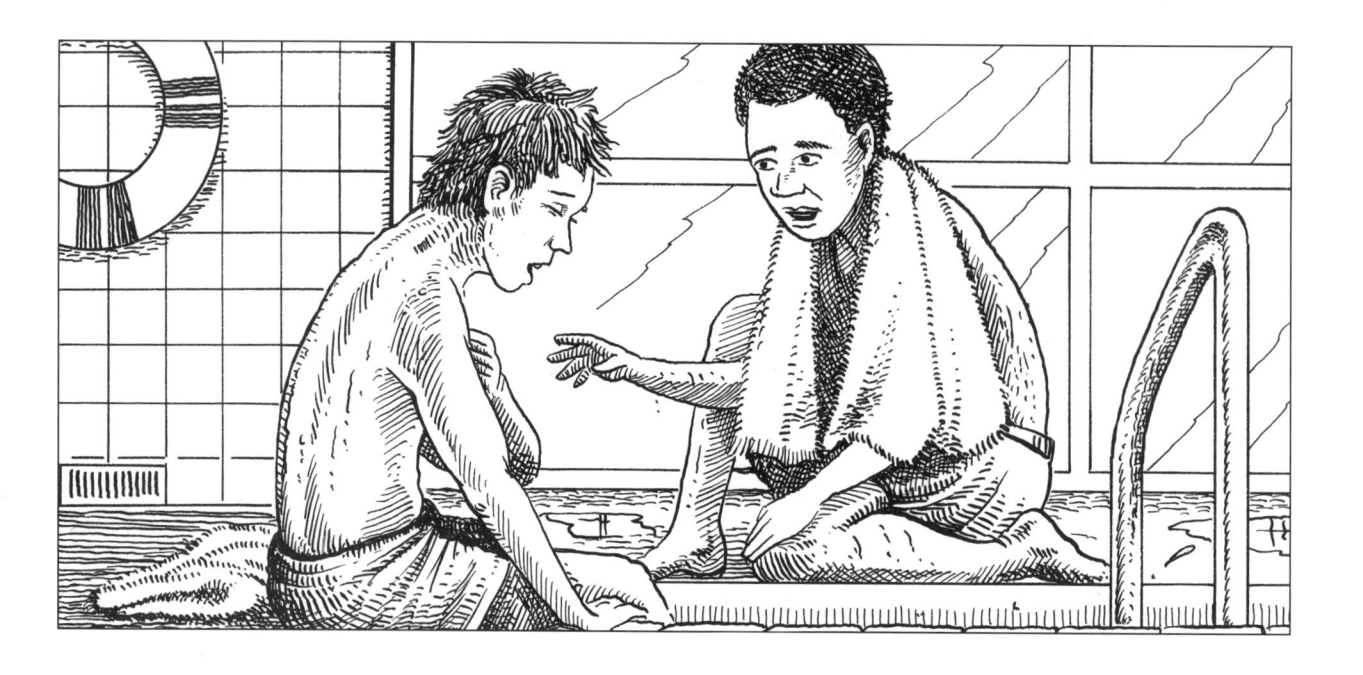

"Look, Marlon, I –" I got no further.

"Hey, Marlon! You on for Daredevil Dive?" Rashid called out.

"Yeah. Coming!" Marlon replied. He turned to me. "See you in a minute." And with that he swam off towards the middle of the pool. I waded over to the steps, the water sloshing around my thighs. I rubbed my eyes, which were still stinging, before climbing out. I turned to where Rashid, Nathan and Andrew were all splashing about. Marlon had just reached them. I didn't want to watch but I couldn't help it. I couldn't bring myself to look away. Instead I sat down at the edge of the pool, my legs dangling in the water as I watched my friends. I sidled a bit closer until I could hear them as well. Kicking out leisurely with my legs, I looked straight ahead, although I was listening to every word Marlon and the others said.

"Everyone ready?" asked Rashid. "OK, let's do it. First one to dive and touch the bottom, then come back and touch the side of the pool wins."

"Ready..."

"Steady..."

"GO!"

In an instant all four boys disappeared under the water. I held my breath as I watched, until my lungs started to ache and my heart started to pound and I couldn't stand it any longer. And still none of my friends had emerged from the water. I gasped, my whole body screaming in angry, pained protest as I concentrated on filling my lungs.

Slow down. I've stopped holding my breath now, I told my heart. Just slow down.

I knew that within the next few weeks I'd no longer be able to come swimming with Marlon and my other friends. I knew it as surely as I knew my own name.

Because my heart was getting worse.

So I had to hang on to these last moments of independence – even if part of it was just fooling myself.

26 Why does the writer, Cam, keep his eyes open?

to stay down	because he can
A	**B**
to avoid a collision	to feel the chlorine
C	**D**

(handwritten: ① beside question; C is circled)

27 Why does the writer put the words 'Silence' and 'Peace' on lines of their own?

A because they are sentences

B to emphasise the contrast with the first paragraph

C because they are speech

D to show that the writer has stopped thinking

(handwritten: 0/B beside question; D is circled)

28 How does Cam feel about the 'angry monster'?

He feels afraid.	He feels defiant.	He will stab it.	He doesn't care.
A	**B**	**C**	**D**

(handwritten: ① beside question; B is circled)

29 'I fought down the urge to apologize.' What does this tell you about Cam?

He is proud but knows he has been rude.	He wants Marlon to apologise.
A	**B**
He hates apologising.	He knows he shouldn't fight.
C	**D**

(handwritten: 0/A beside question; B option scribbled out; D is circled)

30 'But, as always, I caved in.' What does *caved in* mean?

fell down	**submitted**
A	*B*
changed his mind	**carried on**
C	*D*

31 Which description best sums up the relationship between Cam and Marlon?

A They understand each other well.

B They just meet to go swimming.

C They are in the same class at school.

D They belong to the same club.

32 Cam is disappointed that he cannot do the Daredevil Dive. What does he do to hide his feelings?

A He is rude to Marlon.

B He pretends not to listen to the rules.

C He says, "Ready, Steady, Go!"

D He kicks hard.

33 'My lungs started to ache and my heart started to pound.' What does *my heart started to pound* mean?

His heart was thumping in his chest. **A**	His heart was angry. **B**
He cannot breathe. **C**	His heart is weak. **D**

34 What does Cam do after holding his breath?

He screams. **A**	He is angry. **B**
He takes a big breath. **C**	He slows down. **D**

35 Why does Cam go swimming?

because he loves diving **A**	to avoid facing his illness **B**
to prove that he can be independent **C**	to practise swimming **D**

36 The first human heart transplant was performed by a South African ___Surgeon___ in 1967.

sirgen **A**	sirgeon **B**	surgen **C**	surgeon **D**

37 Recent research has made the transplant of animal organs into humans a ___Possibility___.

posibility **A**	possibilitey **B**	possibility **C**	possiblety **D**

CANAL LIFE

Sophie is doing a project on canals. She wrote to ask her grandfather about them. She also read about canals and made some notes.

Dearest Sophie,

Thank you for your letter, full of questions. It sounds a very interesting project you are working on. I'll remember what I can of the life on the canals as my grandfather described it to me.

My grandfather worked hard all his life. The canals were a way of life, not just a job. A barge might begin travelling at 5.30 am and not moor up until 9 pm in the summertime. They had to make use of all available light. And then there would be the horse to take care of.

Before the travelling began the horse would have to be fed and watered and put into the harness, with a similar procedure at the end of the day's work.

Although the work was physically tiring, a boatman would also have to load and unload his own boat with coal, which involved long hours, the wages were poor. In 1919 my grandfather was earning £2 16 shillings and 10d (about £2.84) a week but that might not be every week. If there was nothing to transport, he didn't get paid.

I know my grandmother found life on the barge hard work, but, as she used to say, "at least we're not cooped up in some noisy, overcrowded factory all day." She would sometimes steer the boat while grandfather led the horse along the towpath. If they were hurried, she did even run ahead to prepare the locks for the boat to pass through to save time.

I'll draw you a picture of a lock as it is difficult to explain.

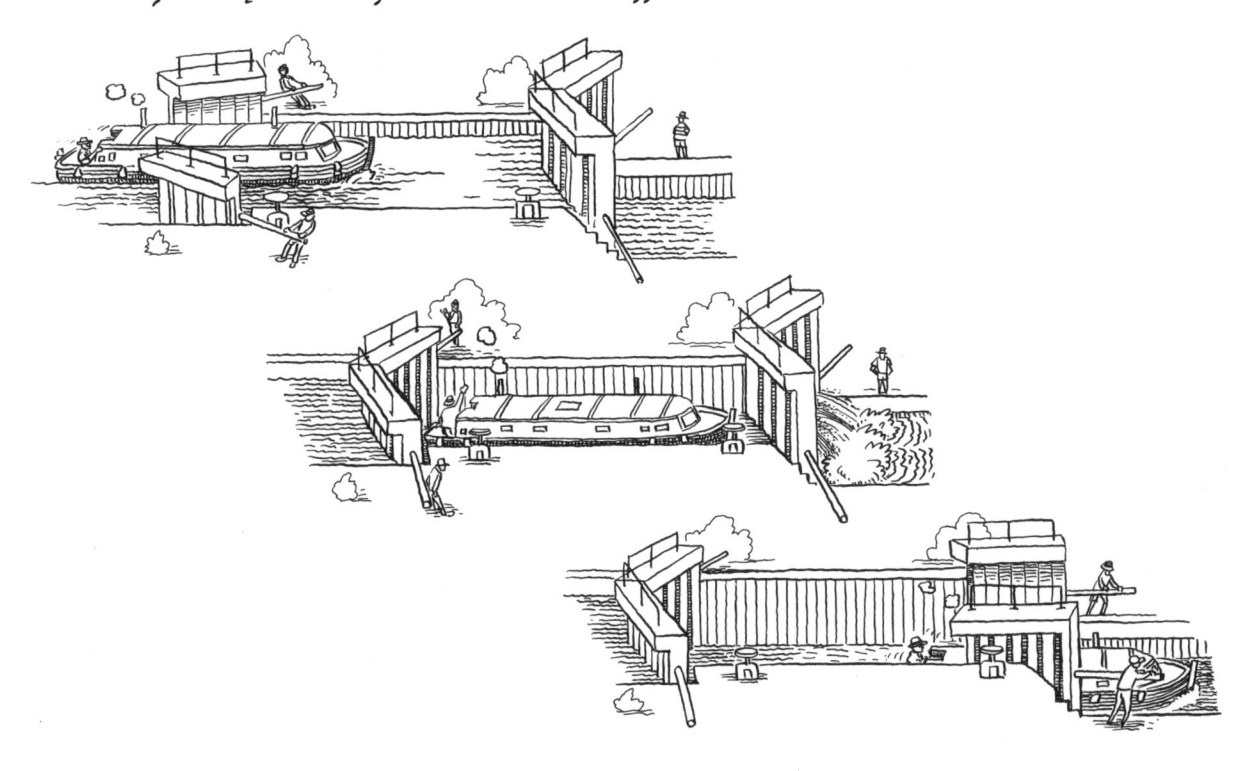

As a child in summer, my father would spend much time on the cabin roof. Not running around, mind you. He would be strapped on so he couldn't fall in the water, but the changing scenery and watching his father work were fascinating, I am sure.

I hope these memories will be of help to you. Let me know how your project turns out.

Good luck
Love Grandad

Sophie wanted to know why people first decided to build canals in the 1700s. These are her notes from the books she read:

◆ People transported their goods in wagons but you would need a lot of horses to pull a heavily-laden wagon, which would be expensive. One barge could transport as much as 60 horses.
◆ The condition of the roads was often very bad with pot holes which could damage your wagon or horses.
◆ It cost money to use sections of the roads. People would have to pay a toll to use the road.
◆ There was a danger of being robbed by a highwayman on isolated lengths of road.

38 This letter is

an invitation.
A

a question.
B

a request.
C

a response.
D

39 Who worked on the barges?

Sophie's grandfather's father
A

Sophie's grandfather's grandfather
B

Sophie's grandmother
C

Sophie's granddaughter
D

40 Why might a day's work begin so early in the summer?

It was a way of life.
A

It would be light.
B

It would be warm.
C

The horse needed feeding.
D

41 '...with a similar procedure at the end of the day's work.'
What does *procedure* mean?

a list
A

a way of harnessing the horse
B

an order or method of doing things
C

what you do at the end of the day
D

42 Name two of the jobs the grandmother might do.

load coal and steer the barge
A

run ahead and cook dinner
B

steer the barge and get the locks ready
C

work in a factory and lead the horse
D

43 You want to give the paragraphs in the letters subheadings. Which is the best heading for the fifth paragraph?

A Woman on the Canal
A

Canal Horses
B

Factories
C

Locks
D

44 "At least we're not cooped up in some noisy, overcrowded factory all day." In the passage, this is an example of

a quotation.
A

an exclamation.
B

a question.
C

indirect speech.
D

45 "At least we're not cooped up in some noisy, overcrowded factory all day." What does *cooped up* mean in the sentence?

packed in
A

sitting
B

stood
C

working
D

46 Sophie has used bullet points in her notes. Why does she use them?

to separate different pieces of information
A

to put her information into numerical order
B

to show each one is a new sentence
C

to show that she read different books
D

47 Which **two** reasons make the canals safer than the roads?

horses and men were expensive
A

tolls and highwaymen
B

pot holes and highwaymen
C

robbery and highwaymen
D

48 Sophie's notes consist mainly of

facts.
A

opinions.
B

suggestions.
C

ideas.
D

49 The Suez Canal is a hundred-mile-long canal _connecting_ the Mediterranean Sea to the Red Sea.

connecting
A

conecting
B

connekting
C

connectting
D

50 The Suez Canal is one of the most important _artificial_ waterways, as it greatly reduces the distance ships have to travel.

artifishel
A

artificial
B

artificel
C

artificail
D

	Understanding the text	Understanding of hidden meaning	Understanding organisation of text	Recognising how language is used	Spelling	Level and success rate
1	A					L4 49%
2		D				L4 37%
3		A				L5 30%
4				D		L4 63%
5	D					L3 74%
6		A				L4 55%
7				B		L5 18%
8	D					L4 63%
9			B			L4 44%
10		C				L3 79%
11		A				L4 45%
12					D	L3 74%
13					C	L4 66%
14	A					L4 48%
15				D		L4 50%
16		C				L4 65%
17			B			L4 36%
18			A			L3 70%
19		D				L5 24%
20	B					L4 64%
21			B			L5 27%
22					B	L2 85%
23					B	L3 73%
24			B			L4 49%
25	A					L4 56%
26	B					L3 67%
27			A			L4 42%
28		C				L3 77%
29			B			L4 52%
30		A				L4 60%
31			B			L3 68%
32				C		L3 69%
33	A					L4 62%
34				D		L5 30%
35		A				L4 39%
36					B	L4 62%
37					C	L2 85%
38					A	L3 74%
39			A			L4 45%
40				C		L5 30%
41	A					L3 71%
42				D		L3 73%
43			A			L3 69%
44	A					L4 63%
45	D					L5 32%
46			C			L4 49%
47				A		L5 32%
48			D			L4 58%
49					D	L3 76%
50					C	L2 82%

Test 1 – How to mark the test

You will need the test booklet, this sheet and a highlighter pen (or an ordinary felt-tip or coloured pencil).

- Open the test booklet at Question 1 and look at the answer your child chose.
- Now find the letter for the correct answer by looking at the first line of the table opposite.
- If the answer chosen for Question 1 is correct, colour the shape in the marking table. If the answer is wrong, leave the shape blank.
- Move on to Question 2 and check the answer in the same way.
- When you have finished marking all the questions in the test, you are ready to find out your child's scores on each type of question.

- Look at the first column of the marking table, called **Understanding the text**.
- Count how many △ shapes in the column are coloured, and write the number in the △ space in the first box below.
- Now count how many ⬭ shapes are coloured, and write the number in the correct space below.
- Now find the total for **Understanding the text** by adding the two numbers (or by counting all the coloured shapes in the first column).
- Do the same for each of the other columns.
- Finally, add up (or count) how many questions in total out of the 50 in the test your child got right. This is the score for the whole test. Now turn to page 49.

Understanding the text

	How many correct
Finding words in the text:	out of 1
Using different words from the text:	out of 7
Total for understanding the text:	out of 8

Understanding of hidden meaning

Drawing conclusions from clues:	out of 5
Understanding characters and situations:	out of 8
Total for understanding of hidden meaning:	out of 13

Understanding organisation of text

Putting events and ideas in order:	out of 2
How text is organised and presented:	out of 8
Total for understanding organisation of text:	out of 10

Recognising how language is used

How words are used:	out of 8
Grammar and punctuation:	out of 3
Total for recognising how language is used:	out of 11

Spelling

Total for spelling:	out of 8

Total for the whole test:	out of 50

	Understanding the text	Understanding of hidden meaning	Understanding organisation of text	Recognising how language is used	Spelling	Level and success rate	
1		A				L3	74%
2			D			L4	51%
3	B					L3	75%
4		A				L3	71%
5				C		L4	63%
6				C		L4	60%
7		C				L3	80%
8				B		L2	85%
9		A				L5	25%
10		D				L4	62%
11					C	L4	59%
12					B	L4	42%
13			C			L4	48%
14	C					L3	70%
15				B		L5	26%
16	C					L4	47%
17				D		L4	50%
18			C			L5	31%
19	D					L4	52%
20				A		L4	43%
21			A			L4	54%
22			B			L4	64%
23			A			L3	70%
24					C	L4	51%
25					A	L4	66%
26	C					L4	54%
27			B			L4	45%
28		B				L5	23%
29		A				L5	31%
30				B		L5	30%
31		A				L4	57%
32		B				L5	22%
33				A		L3	74%
34	C					L4	57%
35		C				L4	45%
36					D	L4	57%
37					C	L4	66%
38		D				L3	69%
39		B				L4	41%
40		B				L4	52%
41				C		L4	57%
42	C					L4	56%
43			A			L4	61%
44				D		L5	29%
45				A		L4	62%
46			A			L3	75%
47	C					L5	31%
48			A			L4	64%
49					A	L3	71%
50					B	L3	77%

altogether in tyt 1 = (16)

Test 2 – How to mark the test

You will need the test booklet, this sheet and a highlighter pen (or an ordinary felt-tip or coloured pencil).

- Open the test booklet at Question 1 and look at the answer your child chose.
- Now find the letter for the correct answer by looking at the first line of the table opposite.
- If the answer chosen for Question 1 is correct, colour the shape in the marking table. If the answer is wrong, leave the shape blank.
- Move on to Question 2 and check the answer in the same way.
- When you have finished marking all the questions in the test, you are ready to find out your child's scores on each type of question.

- Look at the first column of the marking table, called **Understanding the text**.
- Count how many $\triangle$ shapes in the column are coloured, and write the number in the $\triangle$ space in the first box below.
- Now count how many $\bigcirc$ shapes are coloured, and write the number in the correct space below.
- Now find the total for **Understanding the text** by adding the two numbers (or by counting all the coloured shapes in the first column).
- Do the same for each of the other columns.
- Finally, add up (or count) how many questions in total out of the 50 in the test your child got right. This is the score for the whole test. Now turn to page 49.

Understanding the text

How many correct

Finding words in the text:		out of 1
Using different words from the text:		out of 10
Total for understanding the text:		out of 11

Understanding of hidden meaning

Drawing conclusions from clues:		out of 4
Understanding characters and situations:		out of 6
Total for understanding of hidden meaning:		out of 10

Understanding organisation of text

Putting events and ideas in order:		out of 1
How text is organised and presented:		out of 11
Total for understanding organisation of text:		out of 12

Recognising how language is used

How words are used:		out of 4
Grammar and punctuation:		out of 4
Total for recognising how language is used:		out of 8

Spelling

| **Total for spelling:** | | out of 9 |

| **Total for the whole test:** | | out of 50 |

Test 2

Meera Syal

ANITA AND ME

Mama was rummaging about in what we called the Bike Shed, one of two small outhouses at the end of our backyard, the other outhouse being our toilet. We'd never had a bike between us, unless you counted my three-wheeler tricycle which was one of a number of play items discarded amongst the old newspapers, gardening tools, and bulk-bought tins of tomatoes and Cresta fizzy drinks. Of course, this shed should have really been called the bathroom, because it was where we filled an old yellow plastic tub with pans of hot water from the kitchen and had a hurried scrub before frostbite set in, but my mother would have cut out her tongue rather than give it its real shameful name.

"Found it, Mrs Worral!" she shouted from inside the shed. Mrs Worral, with whom we shared adjoining, undivided backyards, stood in her uniform of flowery dress and pinny on her step. She had a face like a friendly potato with a sparse tuft of grey hair on top, and small round glasses, way before they became fashionable, obviously. She moved like she was underwater, slow, deliberate yet curiously graceful steps, and frightened most of the neighbours off with her rasping voice and deadpan, unimpressed face. She did not smile often, and when she did you wished she hadn't bothered as she revealed tombstone teeth stained bright yellow with tobacco smoke. But she loved me, I knew it; she'd only have to hear my voice and she'd lumber out into the yard to catch me, often not speaking, but would just nod, satisfied I was alive and functioning, her eyes impassive behind her thick lenses.

She would listen, apparently enthralled, to my mother's occasional reports on my progress at school, take my homework books carefully in her huge slabs of hands and turn the pages slowly, nodding wisely at the careless drawings and uneven writing. Every evening, when she came to pick up our copy of the *Express and Star* once my papa had finished reading it (an arrangement devised by my mother, "Why should the poor lady have to spend her pension when she can read ours?"), she'd always check up on me, what I was doing, whether I was in my pyjamas yet, whether I was mentally and physically prepared to retire for the night. At least, that's what I read in her eyes, for she never spoke. Just that quick glance up and down, a slight incline of the head, a satisfied exhalation.

1 Which words best describe the writer's bath times?

chilly and quick
A

cramped and dingy
B

frosty and fun
C

rough and hot
D

2 Why would mother have 'cut out her tongue' rather than call the shed a bathroom?

A She doesn't like to be inaccurate.

B It is a mess.

C She is careful to call things by their proper names.

D She is proud and would be embarrassed about it.

3 Mrs Worral wore 'a uniform of flowery dress and pinny'. What does this tell us about her?

She always dressed the same.
A

She had been peeling potatoes.
B

She had just got in from work.
C

She was always smart.
D

4 Which simile in the text describes Mrs Worral's way of walking?

deliberate yet curiously graceful
A

she did not smile often
B

she had a face like a friendly potato
C

she moved like she was underwater
D

5 Why was it a good thing that Mrs Worral did not smile often?

People are unimpressed.
A

She frightens people.
B

She has a rasping voice.
C

She has unpleasant teeth.
D

6 What is Mrs Worral's overall feeling towards the writer?

She cares about her.
A

She is not interested in her.
B

She likes to listen to her school reports.
C

She checks up on her homework.
D

7 Which verb is used to describe Mrs Worral's movement?

deadpan
A

lumber
B

nod
C

slow
D

8 What is the writer's schoolwork like?

careful
A

clever
B

interesting
C

rather untidy
D

9 Why is *Express and Star* written in italics?

because it is two names	**to show it is the name of a publication**
A	*B*
to show it belongs to the family	**to make it stand out**
C	*D*

10 How does the writer know what Mrs Worral was thinking?

because she told her	**because her mother told her**
A	*B*
because of the expression in Mrs Worral's eyes	**because she spoke to her**
C	*D*

11 What impression have you formed of the writer's feelings toward Mrs Worral by the end of the text?

affection	**dislike**	**irritation**	**responsibility**
A	*B*	*C*	*D*

12 Sales of newspapers have been affected by the popularity of the _____television_____ news.

televison	**televesion**	**telivision**	**television**
A	*B*	*C*	*D*

13 A person who researches and writes stories for newpapers is called a _____journalist_____.

jernalist	**journallist**	**journalist**	**journelist**
A	*B*	*C*	*D*

total - 4   I got confused.

Angela Schofield

SHOES

WELL-MADE SHOES PROTECT THE FEET and are also comfortable and long-lasting. The best shoemakers use a wooden or plastic mould, called a last, which matches the shape of the customer's foot. The different parts of a shoe are stitched and glued together around the last; rivets and nails are used only in the heel, which is built up from layers of leather and rubber. The steel shank gives support to the arch of the foot and, with the seat lift, helps the wearer maintain posture. The layers of the sole give strength, while the soft insole cushions the foot. The leather welt sewn between the leather uppers and the sole ensures a strong join.

Cross section of finished shoe

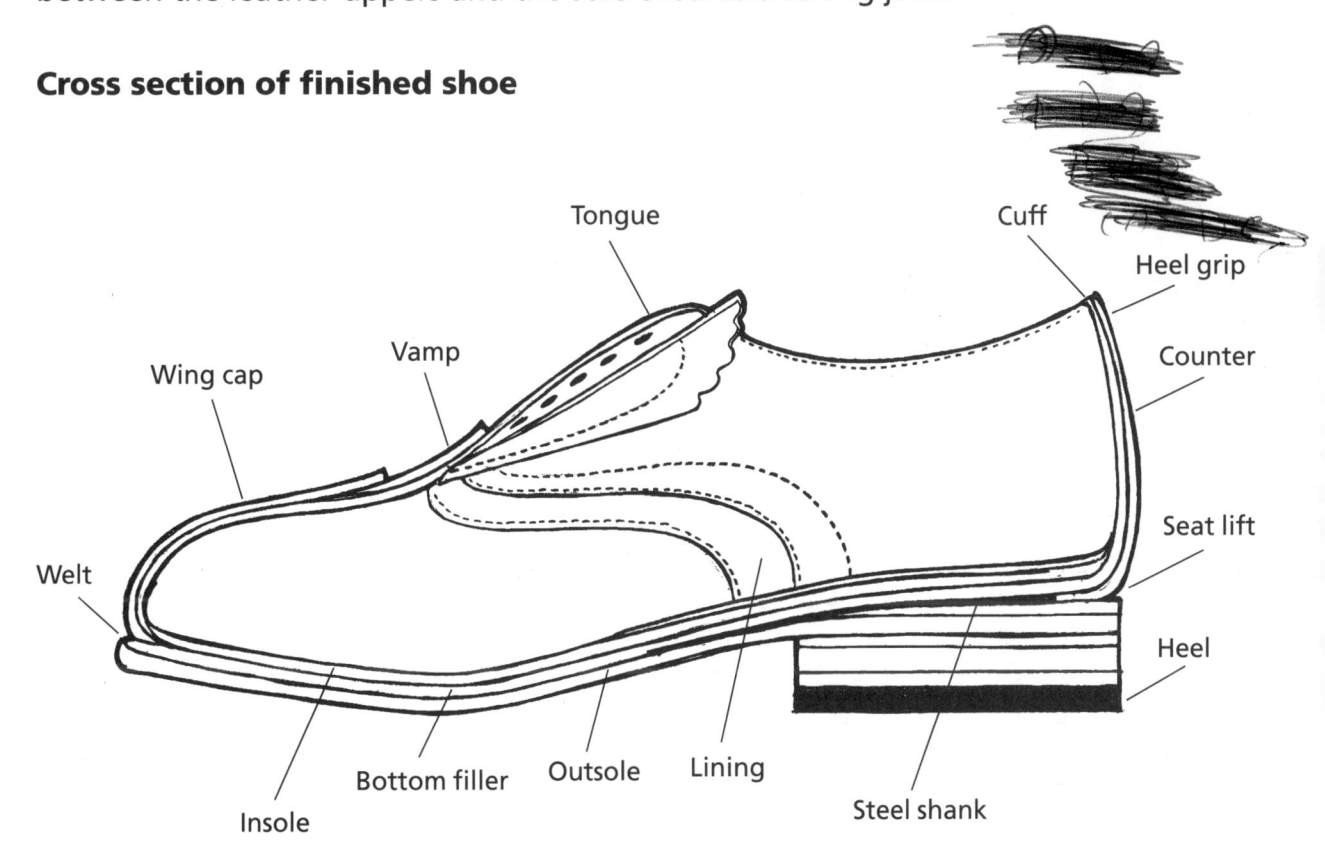

UNCOMFORTABLE SHOES
In the Middle Ages footwear for the rich became very decorative and exaggerated. The pointed toes became longer and longer, stuffed with hay to keep their shape. At last they were so long they had to be fastened to the knee with ribbons! This made walking difficult and kneeling impossible. Eventually, laws were passed to prevent the toes of such shoes getting any longer.

HIGH-HEELED SHOES

During the eighteenth century, ladies shoes were styled with very high heels and pointed toes. Made of wood and covered with rich brocade or brightly-coloured leather they cannot have been very comfortable, especially for walking on cobbled streets! The patterned material was sometimes trimmed with embroidery or even jewels, and fastened usually with a buckle. In wet weather, ladies could wear pattens, to protect their feet and dainty shoes.

SPORTS SHOES

Originally designed for sports wear, the training shoe is increasingly worn as an everyday shoe. The 'trainer' is so popular because it is light, moulded to the foot for comfort, soft and easy to wear. The uppers may be plastic or leather, but the soles are usually made from hard-wearing, man-made materials.

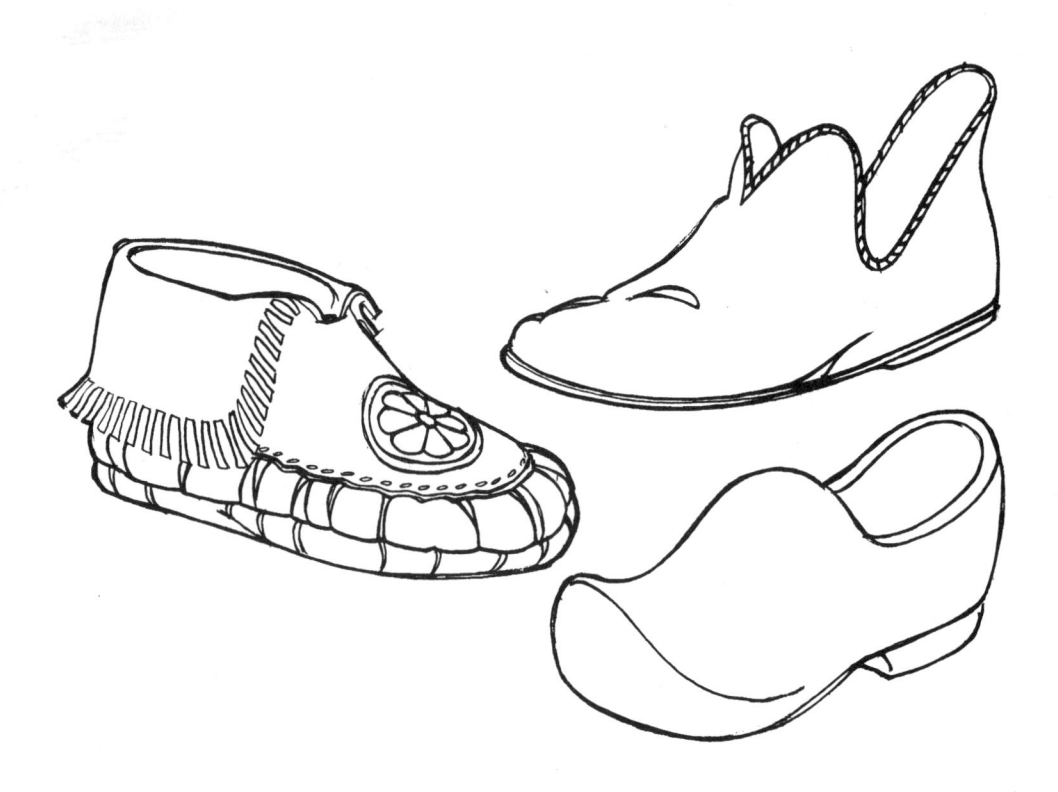

A Guide to Footwear

jackboot	a stiff boot in which the uppers were held up by a metal frame known as a jack
moccasins	soft shoes often made from animal hides as worn by Native Americans
poulaines	long-toed, soft shoes worn in the Middle Ages
sabots	carved wooden shoes

14 What is a *last*?

a model of a foot	a part of the shoe	a pattern for a shoe	a wooden heel
A	**B**	**C**	**D**

15 '...they had to be fastened to the knee with ribbons!' Why does the writer use an exclamation mark?

A because it might be dangerous

B because it is a fact

C because it was against the law

D because the writer finds this ridiculous

16 Why do you think the toes of shoes became so long in the Middle Ages?

A because materials were cheap

B because they were easy to make

C to show how rich and fashionable a person was

D to show how well people could walk

17 All the paragraphs include information on

how to make shoes.	materials used in shoes.
A	**B**
sizes of shoes.	styles of shoes.
C	**D**

18 Which paragraph is related to the diagram on page 31?

1	**2**	**3**	**4**
A	B	C	D

19 What is a *patten*?

a material	**a type of decoration**
A	B
a type of sandal	**something worn over a shoe**
C	D

20 In which period were jewelled shoes worn?

in the twentieth century	**in the eighteenth century**
A	B
in the Middle Ages	**in the nineteenth century**
C	D

21 The word *patten* has to be entered in the *Guide to Footwear*. Which word will it follow?

jackboot	**moccasins**	**poulaines**	**sabots**
A	B	C	D

22 The human foot contains twenty-six bones, _____ fourteen in the toes.

incloding	**including**	**inculding**	**inklooding**
A	B	C	D

23 There are many specialised kinds of shoe designed for _____ activities such as ballet.

leshur	**leisure**	**liesure**	**leasher**
A	B	C	D

Christina Rees

LIVING ON A BOAT

We also learned how to catch fish with a fishing pole as well as with a drop line. I would fasten a small bit of bait, usually some leftover meat from our last meal, and perch as motionless as possible by the railing of the boat. Then I would gently lower the line, and sit with it curled over my index finger, holding the remainder of it in my other hand. Whenever there was a nibble, I could feel it tugging on my index finger. Depending on the strength of the tug, I would respond with a little jerk of my finger or stay motionless and wait for a more substantial bite. I found catching fish to be a great thrill, one of which I never tired. There was something exciting about feeling the line pulling away from me, knowing I had hooked a fish. Sometimes we caught catfish, which we threw back, sometimes we caught flounder, which were very tasty, and sometimes we got the many other types of small fish that inhabited the waterways. Occasionally we would hook something larger and much heavier, but it usually broke the line before we could land it. We had numerous experiences with the one that got away – all true!

Our daily chores were to make our bunks upon rising, fold our night clothes and put them away, and then help Mommy with breakfast, if there was anything we could do, or if not, just stay out of the way. Later we helped Mommy and Daddy with their turns at the helm. We would sit in the cockpit with them, feeling very grown up. In time, we were allowed to adjust the lines if the wind was not too strong. We learned to throw out the anchor and read the currents; we learned about trimming the sails according to the direction of the winds. It was a life totally involved with nature.

We were dependent upon the tides, the depth of the water, the winds and the general weather conditions. If the water was choppy (that is, light waves that throw up a bit of spray and disturb the surface of the water) we knew that we would be in for a bumpy ride, and we knew that it would be more difficult to catch fish. Fish do not like to bite when it is choppy nor when it is too windy. They prefer a nice calm day, and they have feeding times during which they are much more likely to bite.

I remember when I first tried to clean a fish. It seemed impossibly slimy and slippery, and I could not even hold it, much less scale it. At first Daddy or Mommy would kill the fish for me and then let me struggle clumsily as I scraped off the scales. Later I progressed to killing, gutting, and filleting the fish, something that I learned to do within minutes.

I loved fish. I loved to eat them. But mainly I loved to watch them underwater and see their bright colours flashing and their graceful movements. I can remember wishing that I could breathe underwater so that I could swim around with the fish. I think I would have liked to have been a cross between Dr. Dolittle and a mermaid – the best of both worlds.

24 The text is from a book giving an account of the writer's childhood. This is known as

an article.	**an autobiography.**
A	*B*
a biography.	**a novel.**
C	*D*

25 Sometimes the writer decided to 'jerk the line'. What made her decide whether or not to do this?

how hard the fish pulled	**how long she had waited**
A	*B*
how much bait remained	**how quickly her finger jerked**
C	*D*

26 Which fish were pleasant to eat?

catfish	**flounders**
A	*B*
large fish	**small fish**
C	*D*

27 Which of these sentences best describes the content of paragraph 2?

It describes the work she did.	It lists her morning jobs.
A	B

It tells us about her life with nature.	It tells us what she enjoyed.
C	D

28 How did the author feel about doing jobs to help sail the boat?

bored	fed up	proud	worried
A	B	C	D

29 What do the brackets in paragraph 3 contain?

a quotation	an explanation
A	B

an idea	some advice
C	D

30 What does *a bumpy ride* mean?

a difficult or dangerous time	a quick journey
A	B

it is fun	there will not be many fish
C	D

31 The writer's presentation of her story is

arrogant.	**knowledgeable.**
A	B

scientific.	**sentimental.**
C	D

32 Which two words are adjectives used to describe the fish she cleaned?

impossibly and **first**	**killing** and **gutting**
A	B

slimy and **slippery**	**struggle** and **scraped**
C	D

33 To prepare a fish for cooking and eating the writer needed to

remove its scales and insides.	**remove the slime.**
A	B

take out its guts.	**wash it thoroughly.**
C	D

34 Why does the author repeat *loved* in the final paragraph?

because fish are graceful	**by accident**
A	B

for description	**for emphasis**
C	D

35 Which sentence below sums up what the author enjoyed about fishing? Use the whole of the text for your answer.

A She enjoyed the excitement of the catch and the beauty and taste of the fish.

B She loved catching big fish and seeing their colours.

C She enjoyed watching the fish underwater and wanted to be like them.

D She liked the choppy sea and eating the fish.

36 Whales are among the most _____ and graceful of all creatures.

inteligent
A

intelligent
B

entelligent
C

entelligant
D

37 The brain of the sperm whale is the biggest of any mammal, _____ more than ninety newtons.

waying
A

weghing
B

weighing
C

weigheing
D

38 Whales have suffered greatly from hunting by humans, and many kinds are on the official list of _____ species.

endangered *A*	**endagerd** *B*
endangred *C*	**endanjerd** *D*

IT'S SIMPLY MAGIC!

This week's young journalist, Max Britten aged 12, wrote the following for his school newspaper.

Magic in the past

Magic is truly an ancient art. As long ago as 50 000 BC magic was being practised by cave-dwellers, probably as part of their religious rituals. The first written record of a magician giving a performance appears in an ancient Egyptian text, the Westcar Papyrus, from as far back as 2700 BC.

The writer describes a performance by Dedi of Dedsnefu, in which he cut off the head of a duck, a pelican and an ox, and replaced them on the correct animal without harming any of them. What would animal lovers think of that?

It's a secret!

The first rule of magic is that a magician never gives away the secrets of magic.

Obviously, once you know the secret of a trick, it no longer impresses or amazes. It is better for the magician if the audience remain unaware of how a trick is done and so enjoy the surprise of the performance.

Harry Houdini

A magician who truly believed in showmanship and the secrecy of magic was the renowned Harry Houdini who lived from 1874–1926. Although born in Hungary, Houdini grew up in America but became world-famous through his outstanding magical abilities.

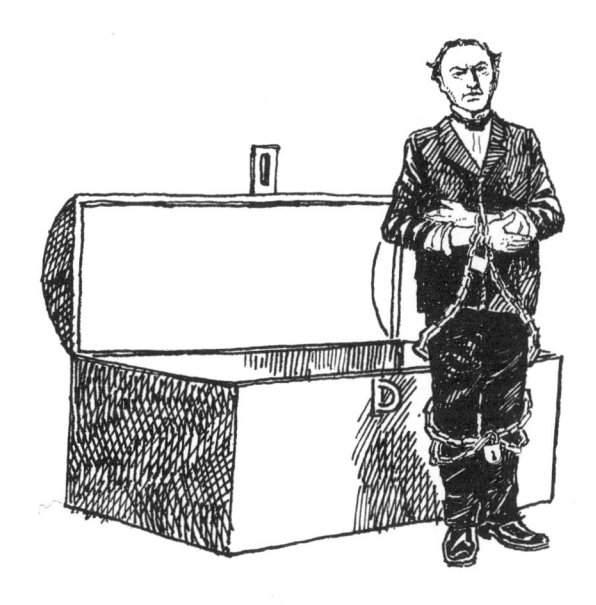

As a skilled escapologist, Houdini could release himself from handcuffs, locked trunks or ropes and would challenge his audience to find ways of binding him. One of his most famous stunts was to escape from a wooden case encircled with steel tape which had been dropped into New York Harbour. He performed the escape in only 59 seconds! (What can *you* do in 59 seconds?)

Magic today

There are many magicians in the world today with at least 10 500 members of the International Brotherhood of Magicians. Thousands more belong to other national organisations.

Other famous magicians and their amazing tricks

Howard Thurston (USA) was famed for his vanishing car.

Percy Tibbles (Britain) was the first to 'saw a woman in half' in 1921.

Sigfried Fischbecker (Germany) could make a person float in air.

ACTION STATIONS!

If you are a keen magician, you could contact your local magicians' association (get the number from your telephone directory). Or, why not set up a club at your school to exchange tricks with other crafty conjurors?

Did you know?
Prestidigitator is another word for a magician – meaning someone who is incredibly quick with their hands.

39 The first paragraph

introduces the writer of the article.	**is a summary.**
A	B
is written by Max.	**tells you how to do magic.**
C	D

40 The apostrophe in the first sentence, 'This week's young journalist...' is used to show

a letter is missing.	**contraction.**
A	B
possession.	**there is an *s*.**
C	D

41 Why should a magician not tell anybody the secret of the magic?

The audience will enjoy it less.	**The magician will not be amazed.**
A	B
The trick will not work.	**There is a law against telling.**
C	D

42 Houdini escaped 'from a wooden case encircled with steel tape'. What does *encircled* mean?

decorated	**with circles on**
A	B
escaped	**wrapped around**
C	D

43 Why does the writer ask the question 'What can *you* do in 59 seconds?'

He wants you to think.	He wants you to break the record.
A	**B**
He wants you to hold your breath.	He wants you to write an answer.
C	**D**

44 Which magician could make a person rise from the ground using magic?

Fischbecker	Houdini
A	**B**
Thurston	Tibbles
C	**D**

45 How many magicians are there today?

a brotherhood	less than 10 500	10 500	more than 10 500
A	**B**	**C**	**D**

46 How many suggestions are given for keen young magicians?

0	1	2	3
A	**B**	**C**	**D**

47 Look at the definition of *prestidigitator*. If the first part of the word, 'presti', refers to speed, what do you think the second part, 'digitator', refers to?

fingers	magic	magician	quick
A	**B**	**C**	**D**

48 This article focuses mainly on

A advice for young magicians.

B famous magicians and their tricks.

C magic tricks and ideas.

D the history of magic and some famous magicians.

49 Magicians throughout history have performed _____ tricks.

incredeble	incredibel
A	B

incredibl	incredible
C	D

50 It is the magician's ability to _____ reality which is so amazing.

traansform	transfoam
A	B

transform	transforme
C	D

How the tests were developed

To develop a sound test, it is important to try out the questions properly and to use the information from the trial to improve the material.

Trying out the tests

Each of the tests in this series was tried out with approximately 400 children of the correct age, and 400 children one year older. The tests were trialled in a wide range of schools across the country. In total, 56 schools took part in trialling the English and mathematics tests, so you can be sure that this group of pupils was similar to other children throughout England.

Number of children whose results were analysed

	Year 3	Year 4	Year 5	Year 6
Mathematics	706	778	752	1051
English	716	947	1021	1106

When the tests were first written, they included extra questions, in case any did not work properly. The trials in schools allowed the developers to include only those questions that performed well.

The trials also gave important information on how children did on different kinds of question. This information has been used to help you compare how well your child is doing with other children of a similar age. You can tell the skill areas in which he or she is successful, or whether help or extra practice is needed. We are also able to give you information about:

- how your child's marks relate to the National Curriculum levels at Key Stage 2
- the National Curriculum level of each question in the test
- the success rate for each question (the number of children of the correct age who got the question right in the trial).

Calibrating the tests

Calibrating a test is like putting the marks on a ruler: it is essential to put them in the right place. The school trial was carefully designed so that the developers could compare children's scores with reliable information on national standards and so set the levels in these tests accurately. The method was to 'cascade' standards down through the years, using similar statistical models to those used in developing national tests. The diagram on the next page shows how this was done.

Year 6 children (Age 10–11)

Year 4 test   Year 5 test   Year 6 test

Children in Year 6 (age 10–11) took a *Level Boosters* Year 6 test and either a Year 5 or a Year 4 test as well.

At the end of the year, these children also took national Key Stage 2 tests in English and Mathematics. Their results were compared directly with the *Level Boosters* tests for Years 4, 5 and 6, and from this comparison the level standards of the *Level Boosters* questions were set.

Year 5 children (Age 9–10)

Year 4 test   Year 5 test

Because the same Year 4 and 5 tests taken by Year 6 children were also taken by children of the right age, the levels set for the Year 6 children could be 'passed down' to those year groups.

Year 4 children (Age 8–9)

Year 4 test   Year 3 test

In Year 4, children took a *Level Boosters* Year 3 and 4 test. This allowed the level standards to be passed down further to Year 3.

Year 3 children (Age 7–8)

Year 3 test

How did your child do?

When you have marked the test using the marking sheet, you are ready to find out how well your child did. To find out how his or her performance compared with other children of the same age, check the score for the test below.

Test 1

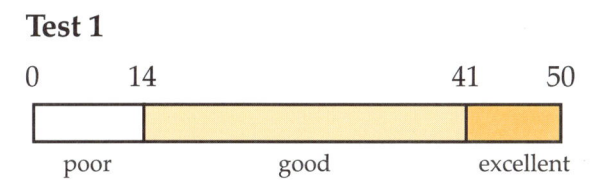

Test 2

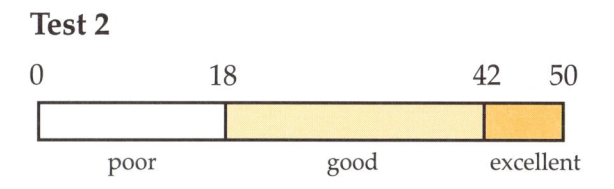

The tables below enable you to compare how well your child has done with the levels in the Key Stage 2 National Curriculum test of English.

Test 1

Score	Level
0–11	level 2 or below
12–22	level 3
23–34	level 4
35–50	level 5 or above

Test 2

Score	Level
0–10	level 2 or below
11–22	level 3
23–36	level 4
37–50	level 5 or above

> **To the child**
> Did you do as well as you hoped? Perhaps there are some particular areas of English that you could work on to improve your score. Look at the charts on the next page to find out how you did in each area.

The bar charts opposite show how to judge your child's performance in each area of English covered in Test 1 and Test 2. There are three categories of performance, just as there are for the overall level of achievement on the tests:

Excellent This is an outstanding achievement. To reach this standard your child will have correctly answered the level 3 and level 4 questions and succeeded with many of the level 5 questions, which are the hardest in the test. The charts show that only some areas of English have questions that are very hard and which, over the whole test, only the most able third of all the children in the trial answered correctly.

Good To reach this standard your child is most likely to be answering the level 3 questions correctly and is getting a number of level 4 questions and possibly some level 5 questions right as well. The majority of children in the trial scored in this range. Check your child's actual score against the bar chart; the higher up the bar, the better your child is doing in this area of English.

Poor This indicates that your child has most likely succeeded only with some of the easiest questions, the level 2 and 3 questions. These were answered correctly by at least two-thirds of all the children in the trial.

There may be a number of reasons why your child has got a question wrong. Once you know which answers are incorrect, the most important step is to help your child learn from his or her mistakes. The information on page 51 explains how to do this.

How well did your child do in each area of English?

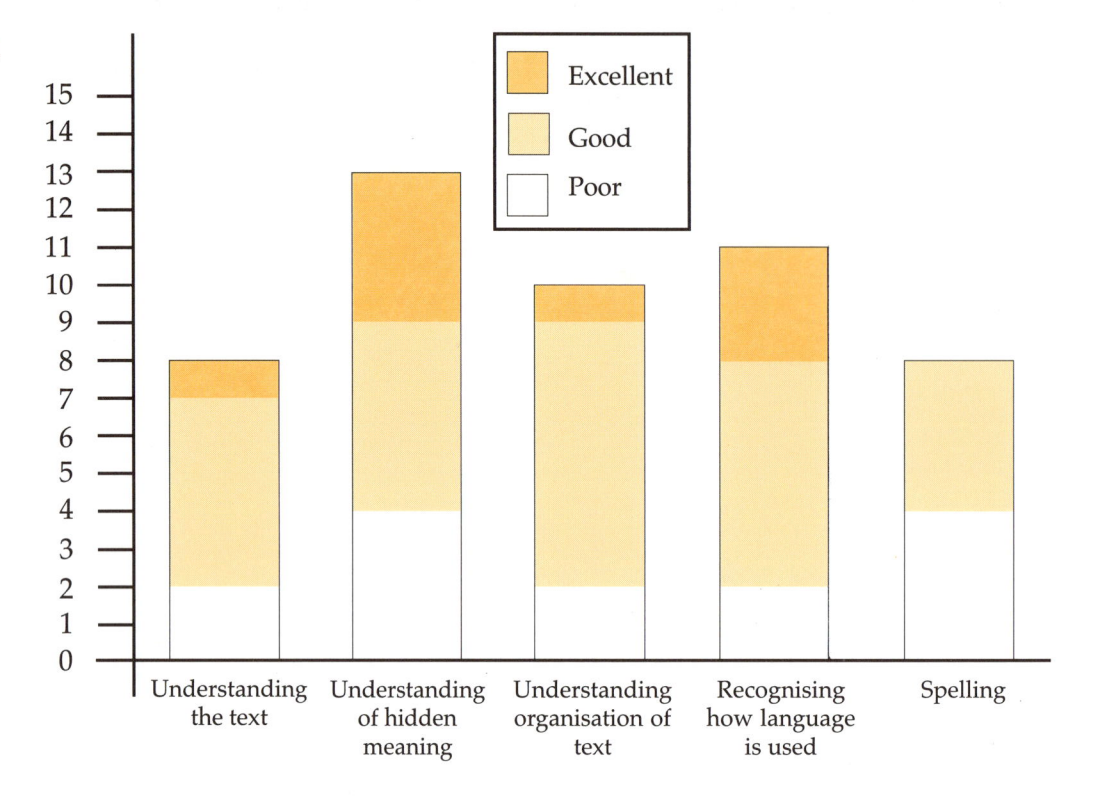

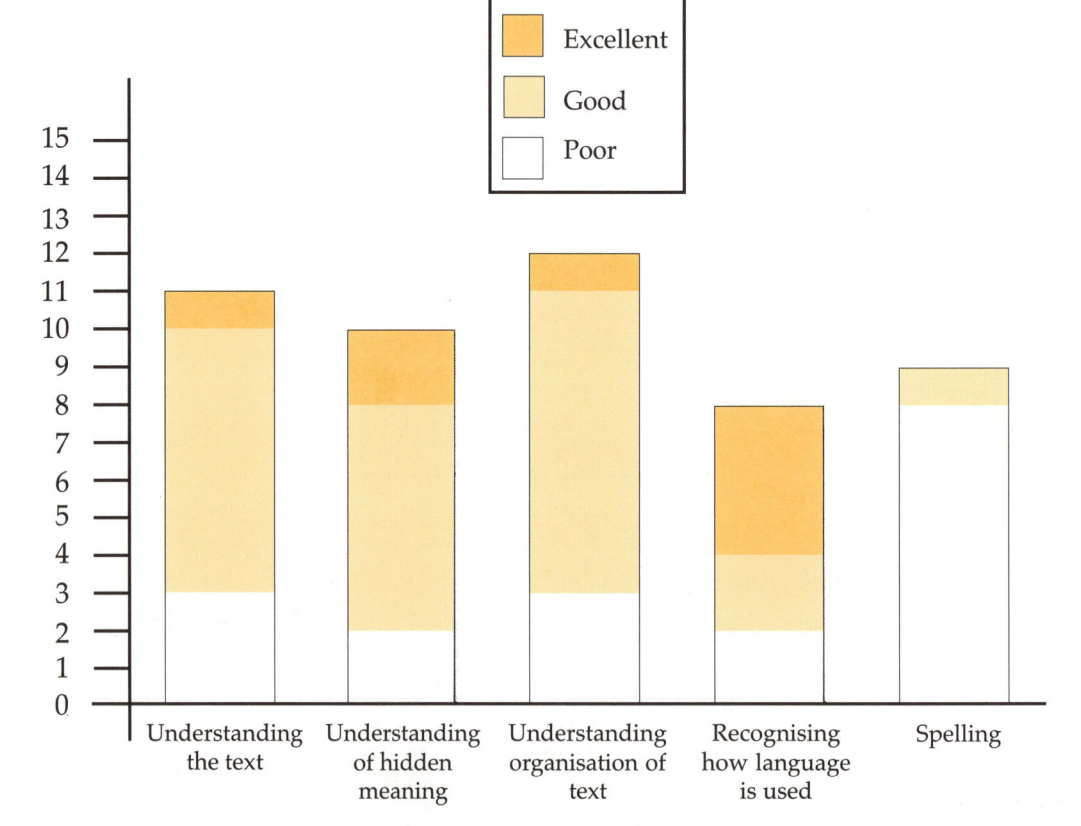

Understanding your child's results and helping them learn how to improve!

Each column on the marking sheet shows the questions on a key skill, such as **Understanding the Text**. Each key skill is then broken down into two types of skill area.

For example, **Understanding the Text** is divided into:

△ finding words in the text. This is finding the same word in the text that appears in the answer.

◯ using different words from the text. This is finding the words that mean the same as words in the question.

Each question in the test assesses a skill area from one column. The shapes you highlighted around the answers show which questions your child got correct in each column. This allows you to see which skill areas your child is good at and which he or she needs more practice on.

For example, in **Understanding the Text**, If your child tended to get the ovals ◯ wrong but the triangles △ right then you know that your child is having problems with 'using different words from the text'.

Helping your child to learn how to improve

Sometimes your child may have made a mistake on a question to which they know the answer. This can happen because of rushing or not reading a question carefully. If you think this is the case, point out the error and see if your child can correct the answer themselves. However, there may be other reasons for not getting the right answers. You could ...

Step 1. Check that your child understands the question.

Step 2. Ask him or her to show you where they think the answer comes from in the passage.

Step 3. Explore with him or her why they chose the answer they did. Ask if there are any other words in the text which make them think a different answer could be right.

Step 4. If they are still lost show them the correct answer and talk about why it is correct.

How to Check

Suppose your child got four marks for **Understanding of Hidden Meaning**. When you look at the highlighted shapes on the answer sheet you notice that three of these marks were for questions where he or she had to draw conclusions from clues, shown by △, and two marks were for understanding characters and situations, shown by ◯. Here is an example of how one girl worked out why she had got *Question 34* wrong in Test 1. The question asked, 'How does Cam feel about the 'angry monster'?'

- She had found the 'angry monster' in the text and, in the same place, found the words 'sharp, stabbing pain' and 'screamed'. She had imagined how she would feel if she were Cam and circled, 'he feels afraid' as the answer.
- Together she and her father looked to see what the correct answer was. The answer she should have given was, 'he feels defiant'.
- They looked back at the text to see how she could have know that Cam felt defiant and not afraid. She found the same place in the text but read it more slowly and carefully. This time she saw that after the 'angry monster' description Cam said, 'it would be at my own pace and in my own time ... I was the one in control'. He was saying that he would not be afraid or beaten by the blood that roared in his ears like an angry monster.

Your next step

Together look back at your child's marking sheet and follow the above steps.

About the writing team

These tests are the brainchild of Dr Colin McCarty. As director of a wide range of National Curriculum test development projects, he has come to see that when children take tests, not only do they show us how well they are doing, but also there is a great opportunity for them to learn from their mistakes. He is also aware that teachers are doing an excellent job but would value more help from parents.

These tests were written to support parents in helping their children do better and so improve the partnership between pupils, parents and professionals.

The English tests have been written and developed by a team of consultants working for the Research Division of the University of Cambridge Local Examinations Syndicate (UCLES). They are:

Judy Abbott, **Kathma Dawson**, **Lesley Densham**, **Nick Hillman**, **Marie Lallaway** and **Sarah Maughan**.

Each consultant has been involved in aspects of the development of the Years 3, 4 and 5 Optional Tests in English for the Qualifications and Curriculum Authority (QCA). The optional tests are used in many primary schools to assist teachers measure the progress of their pupils. The consultants undertook the analysis of pupil performance nationally on the optional tests in 1998 and 1999 and their findings have been reported to schools by QCA.

The writing and development programme and the test trialling have been directed by Dr Colin McCarty of UCLES. The Publisher is Dr Steve Sizmur, who joined Folens in 1998 from the National Foundation for Educational Research, where he was responsible for a range of primary National Curriculum and test development projects.

The tests are jointly published by Folens, a major schools book publisher, and OCR. OCR (Oxford, Cambridge and RSA Examinations) is the UK division of UCLES and is a foremost GCSE, GNVQ and A Level examining board.

Acknowledgements

First published 2000 by Folens Limited, Dunstable and Dublin, in conjunction with OCR, Cambridge.

Folens Limited, Albert House, Apex Business Centre, Boscombe Road, Dunstable, LU5 4RL, England.

© 2000 Folens Limited and UCLES.

Editor: Gaynor Spry

Layout artist: Patricia Hollingsworth

Cover design: Ed Gallagher

Illustrations: Bob Farley (Graham-Cameron Illustration), Brian Hoskin (Simon Girling Associates), Brian Lee (Graham-Cameron Illustration), Liz McIntosh (Linda Rogers Associates), Trevor Parkin (Linda Rogers Associates).

Text: Page 7–8: Extract from *The Kingdom by the Sea* by Robert Westall (Mammoth). Page 12–13: Reproduced from *Crazy Kites* by Peter Eldin (Arrow Books). Text copyright © 1990 Data Forum Ltd. Page 17–18: © Oneta Malorie Blackman 1997. Extracted from *Pig Heart Boy* by Malorie Blackman, published by Doubleday, a division of Transworld Publishers Ltd. All rights reserved. Page 27: Extract from *Anita and Me* by Meera Syal (HarperCollins Publishers Ltd). Page 31–32: Reproduced from *Clothes in History* by Angela Schofield (Wayland Publishers). Page 35-36: Extract from *Sea Urchin* by Christina Rees (North River Press).

Every effort has been made to contact copyright holders of material used in this book. If any have been overlooked, we will be pleased to make any necessary arrangements.

British Library Cataloguing in Publication Data. A catalogue record for this book is available from the British Library.

ISBN 1 84163 329–1

Printed in the United Kingdom by WM Print.